IMAGES
of Ireland

AROUND
DUNGANNON

The Old Cross at Donaghmore.

IMAGES
of Ireland

AROUND
DUNGANNON

Compiled by
Felix Hagan

GILL & MACMILLAN

Published in Ireland by
Gill & Macmillan Ltd
Goldenbridge, Dublin 8
with associated companies throughout the world
Copyright © Felix Hagan, 1998

ISBN 0 7171 2851 2

Typesetting and origination by
Tempus Publishing Limited
Printed in Great Britain by
Midway Clark Printing, Wiltshire

The Dungannon Bar, seen here at the turn of the century, stood at the point where Ann Street joined Irish Street. The site is now occupied by Carmel's boutique and the new Thomas Street to William Street thoroughfare.

Contents

Acknowledgements

The author wishes to express his gratitude to all the people who have helped him in this work: Ms Pat McLean of the Ulster Museum, Belfast, and Mr David McLaughlin of the National Library of Ireland, Dublin, for their assistance and advice; to all who have lent the photographs used, including: Mr Iain Fraser and Dungannon District Council, along with those who donated the photographs to the council; Richard Dilworth, Moygashel; Dermot Cavanagh, Dungannon; Fred Kullas, Coalisland; Mrs Frizelle, Dungannon; Eric Maginnis, Canada; Miss Finnella Finney, Dungannon; Mrs Bertha Hadden, Dungannon; Mrs Ella Mills, Dungannon; Mr Jim Robinson, Dungannon; Mr Tony Corr, Pomeroy; Mr Paddy Mulgrew, Dungannon; Mrs Margaret McGinty, Dungannon; Mrs Helen McRory and Sister M. Brogan, St Joseph's Convent Grammar School, Donaghmore; Mr P.J. Rafferty, Donaghmore; Mr Norman Cardwell, Royal School, Dungannon; Mr Oliver Corr, Coalisland Heritage Trust; Brother Joseph, Servite Priory, Benburb; Mr Pat Tally, Galbally Pearses' GFC; Mrs Noeleen Mullin, Benburb Valley Heritage Centre; Mrs Frances Glasgow, Ballytrea PS; Mrs Barbara Cuddy and Mrs Brenda Rollins, Walker Memorial PS, Castlecaulfield; Mrs Doreen McIntyre and Miss Mairead O'Neill, St Brigid's PS, Brocagh; Mrs Heather Griffin, Drumsallen PS, Benburb; Mr Robert Trimble, Moy Regional PS; Mr Sean McMorrow, Roan PS; Mr Colin McClure and Mrs Mildred Jackson, Killyman PS; Mr Patrick Mallon, Our Lady's PS, Tullysaran; Mr Gerry Kelly, Laghey PS; Mrs Carole Lawson, Tullyroan PS; Mrs Sandra Richardson, Newmills PS; Mr Barry Randall, Clintyclay PS; Mr James Logan, Edendork PS; Mr Tom Jordan, St John's PS, Kingsisland; Mrs Chris O'Neill, Aughamullan PS; Mr Peter McGrath, St Patrick's PS, Dungannon; Mr Melvyn Hull, Tamnamore PS; Mr Tommy Cuddy, Stewartstown; Mrs Kate Wilson; Mr Kenneth Sharkey; Miss Emma Dickson; Mr Alexander Condy, Lisfearty PS; Mr John Rea, St Mary's PS, Cabra; Mrs Mary McGinley, St Patrick's Girls' High School, Dungannon; Mr Louis Campbell, Coalisland; Mr Seamus Lynch, Donaghmore; Mr Philip Dynes, Dungannon; Mr Ciaran MacAoidh, Eoghan Ruadh Hurling Club, Dungannon; Mr Dick Agnew, Dungannon Golf Club; Mr Glyn Dodds, Loughgall FC; Mr David Gallagher and Mr David Holmes, Dungannon Swifts FC; Mr Philip Orr, Dungannon Cricket Club; Mrs Dolores Morgan, Derrylaughan St Patrick's Camogie Club; Mrs Marie Toland, Clonoe St Ann's and Kingsisland St Colmcille's Camogie Clubs; Mrs Maura Doris, Washingbay; Mrs Ursula Jordan, Eglish St Teresa's Camogie Club; Mr Harold Walker, Dungannon RFC; Mr Patsy Gallagher, Donaghmore St Patrick's GFC; Mr Pearse Kelly, Brackaville Owen Roe's GFC; Mr Oliver McHugh, Dungannon, Thomas Clarke's GFC; Mr Terry McShane, Killyman St Mary's GFC; Mr Frankie Duffy, Moy Tír na nÓg GFC; Mr Conor Daly, Eglish St Patrick's GFC; Mr Brian Duffin, Clonoe O'Rahilly's GFC; Mr Martin O'Neill, Brocagh Emmett's GFC; Mr Brian McLernon, Derrylaughan Kevin Barry's GFC; Mr Gerard Ryan, Derrytresk Fir-an-Chnuic GFC; Mr Ronan Park, Stewartstown Harps GFC; Mr Sean Begley and Mr Michael McGeary, Pomeroy Plunketts' GFC; Mr John Ward, Rock St Patrick's GFC; Mr Plunkett Begley, Pomeroy; and all my fellow members of the committee of Donaghmore Historical Society for their encouragement.

And finally to Ruth and Trevor and to all at CR Print, Dungannon, for courtesy, patience and efficiency at all times.

Introduction

The name 'Dungannon' is derived from Genan, son of Cathbad the druid, one of the Red Branch Knights, who dwelt beside the royal court of Emain Macha (modern Armagh) and was friend of the legendary Ulster hero, Cuchulainn, and the word *dún* which in Gaelic means 'a fort'. Genan built a fort on the hill of what has become the modern town of Dungannon. However, the recorded history of Dungannon really begins in the fourteenth century when the O'Neills, Princes of Ulster, moved there from nearby Tullyhogue. With the defeat of Hugh O'Neill's forces at the Battle of Kinsale in 1601 and his departure from Ireland in the Flight of the Earls in 1607, Dungannon ceased to be a royal seat.

Following the Williamite Wars in the late seventeenth century, Dungannon was purchased by the Knox family from Belfast. Thomas Knox, the third generation of this family in Dungannon, was created Baron Welles in 1781 and Viscount Northland in 1791. His son, also Thomas, was created Baron Ranfurly in 1826 and the first Earl of Ranfurly in 1831. The family residence, Northland House, was built in 1785. The Ranfurly Knoxes left Dungannon in 1927, the residence was sold and demolished, and is now the rugby pitch of the Royal School.

Dungannon hosted the Volunteer Convention of 1782. The United Irishman, Thomas Russell, known as 'The Man from God Knows Where', was appointed to the position of Seneschal of Dungannon and a magistrate while another United Irish leader of the same period, Henry Joy McCracken, who like Russell was hanged for his involvement, also lived there. Thomas J. Clarke, the first signatory of the Proclamation of the Irish Republic in 1916, spent most of his youth in Dungannon.

Donaghmore – in Gaelic 'the big church' – lies three miles north-west of Dungannon. It was an early monastic settlement, where St Patrick founded an abbey in the fifth century. The ancient Celtic cross (see p. 2), a composite of two crosses, which stands at the top of the village's main street, dates from the ninth century. In the late eighteenth century Alexander MacKenzie founded a brewery here which flourished for over a hundred years, while in the 1820s David Brown set up a soap-making business which by the end of the century was the largest in Ireland. It later declined as by the 1950s it could no longer compete with the mass-producing companies. Revd George Walker, Governor of Derry during the city's siege in 1689, and who was killed at the Battle of the Boyne the following year, was once rector of Donaghmore as was Revd Charles Wolfe who wrote the stirring *The Burial of Sir John Moore at Corunna*.

Nearby is Castlecaulfield where Sir Toby Caulfield built his castle in the early seventeenth century. His former residence, Parkanaur House, was acquired by the Burges family in the late eighteenth century. Pomeroy, the second highest village in Ireland, nine miles north-west of Dungannon, has been associated with the Lowry family since the mid-eighteenth century. Coalisland, as the name suggests, is one of the few places in Ireland which had a coal-mining industry. It is four miles from Dungannon and was linked to the Ulster Canal. Some mining took place here from the early eighteenth century but by the 1950s it had petered out. Moy, five miles south-east of Dungannon, had one of the leading horse fairs in Europe in the last century and the early part of this century, until the horse's role as a farm animal ended. Benburb, eight miles south of Dungannon, is famous for its castle. In the surrounding area are the sites of two battles: the Battle of the Yellow Ford where in 1598 Hugh O'Neill, Earl of Tyrone, overcame Sir Henry Bagenal and, almost half a century later, the place where his nephew, Owen Roe O'Neill, beat a Scottish army under General Robert Munro at the Battle of Benburb.

Wiggins's Hill from the Donaghmore road.

One
Dungannon

A general view of Dungannon from Beechvalley early in the twentieth century.

The coat of arms of Dungannon.

Market Square at the turn of the century. The only parking problems were caused by carts. No painted lines were necessary on the cobbled streets.

Market Square from the Irish Street end on a busy market day.

Ann Street in the early years of the century.

Motor traffic had begun to appear in Ann Street in the 1950s.

The Rat's Pad, off Ann Street, like the street itself, has now disappeared.

A crowded Irish Street around 1900.

In the 1950s is was still legal to drive along Irish Street in either direction.

The Coffee House in Scotch Street in 1906 before the car parks were needed.

An almost deserted George's Street in the latter part of the last century.

Kettle's election rooms in William Street were a focus of much attention during the election campaign of 1906.

Sloan Street as it looked in the middle part of this century before so many of the houses on the left-hand side were pulled down.

Perry Street and Church Street were wide enough for the demands that traffic made upon them in 1869.

Perry Street and Church Street had become busier by the 1950s.

Milltown in the early twentieth century.

The Earl and Countess of Ranfurly in September 1925.

The entrance gate to Northland House, the home of the Ranfurly family.

The front entrance to Northland House.

The lawns at Northland House.

A group at Northland House in 1923 during the visit of the New Zealand Premier. Lord Ranfurly had been Governor General of New Zealand from 1897 to 1904. From left to right, back row: Major Alexander, Lord Charlemont, Lord Ranfurly, -?-, Lady Charlemont, Hon. Rachel Caulfield, Sir Toby Caulfield. Front row: Lady Massey, Sir William F. Massey, Lady Ranfurly.

An agricultural show in Ranfurly Park in the 1920s.

The Black Lough was frozen over in the severe winter of 1940.

Skating on the Black Lough in 1940 is Mr Tom Fox with his two daughters, Mary (in the centre) and Margaret. Margaret is now Mrs Jack McGinty.

The old church of St Anne, which dated from 1607.

The Presbyterian church in Scotch Street which was the scene of the Volunteer Convention of 1782.

St Patrick's Catholic church, which was built in 1868. The freestone used came from the local Carland, Gortnaglush and Bloomhill Quarries. The building of the tower and spire was completed in 1883.

St Patrick's church as seen from the lawn of the Convent of Mercy.

The Convent of Mercy before the monkey-puzzle was planted in the lawn.

St Patrick's Boys' and Girls' Academies stood on the Killyman Road from the 1890s until they were demolished to make way for the new St Patrick's Primary School. The statue of St Patrick is on the front wall.

The Technical Institute, like Ann Street in which it stood, is now gone. How may little girls, like the one in the centre, play with hoops nowadays?

Dungannon House, which later became Drumglass Hospital.

The Belfast Bank (now Irish World) in the Market Square, as it looked in the early 1920s when ivy covered much of its front.

The old Dungannon workhouse with
what was then the new hospital in the
background in the 1960s. Now the South
Tyrone Hospital also faces closure.

Lady Ranfurly unveils the War Memorial
at Market Square in November 1922.

Only one woman, standing close to the centre in a white dress and black jacket, appears to be in attendance at the opening of the reservoir at Castle Hill in 1930. The ruins of O'Neill's Castle provide a historic background.

Lord Ashbourne prepares to lead the Feis Parade from McAleer's Hotel in the mid-1930s. Those present are, from left to right: Jack Fairbairn, Eva McAleer, -?-, Lord Ashbourne, Katie McAleer, -?-, Joe Stewart MP, Vincent Quinn (local Gaelic League), Paddy McNamee (Comhaltas Uladh).

Lord Northland looks on as VE Day is celebrated with a march through Market Square in 1945.

Adults and children queue up for admission to a circus in Ann Street, c. 1950.

Many circus people and locals attended the funeral of Mrs Duffy in Drumcoo cemetery in August 1939. She was the wife of the circus proprietor and, in the tradition of travelling showpeople, she was buried in the town where they were performing at the time of her death.

Resting on Castle Hill in the first half of the twentieth century.

A group gathered at the back of Pat McNaney's shop (now Denis McNaney's chemist's) in the 1930s. From left to right, back row: -?-, Joe Goodwin, Pat McNaney, Joe Campbell (grocer), Willie McNaney, -?-. Front row: Bob Donaghy (cobbler), -?-, -?-, Jimmy Quinn, Matt Donaghy. The notice reads: 'Boots, Shoes and Slippers. Leather Boots, Slippers and Clogs. Handmade Boots. Grocery Dept. John McNaney and Sons.'

Preparation for new buildings in Church Street in 1878.

The office at Stevensons' Warehouse in George's Street in the early 1920s.

At the opening of Smith's Bakery in George's Street in the 1930s. Included in the group are Joe Stewart MP, Rowley Elliott MP, Robert Leith and Alan Dickie.

The horse-drawn van of Filbin Bros, the Lurgan Bakery firm, was a common sight around Dungannon before the Second World War.

Female employees of the munitions factory at Milltown, with their instructor, during the Second World War.

Thomas Street in 1890.

A long-distance view of the Donaghmore Road and Charlemont Street section of the town. The rounded façade of St Patrick's Intermediate School can be seen in the background.

Two
Dungannon District

An unidentified person studies the Cross at Donaghmore with St Patrick's church and Brown's factory chimney in the background.

Donaghmore Old Cross, *c*. 1900.

The 'Bottom Bar' with a
considerable covering of ivy, *c*. 1900.

The Royal Irish Constabulary in Donaghmore at the end of the nineteenth century. Donaghmore lost its barracks in the 1920s.

Two mounted RIC men guard the former St Patrick's National School, now the Heritage Centre.

The Backford Bridge, Donaghmore, around the beginning of the twentieth century.

The Brewery Yard in Donaghmore before Mackenzie's – later Lyle's – Brewery ceased to function in the early years of the twentieth century.

The Donaghmore House gatehouse on the Castlecaulfield Road – it is still standing, but is now unoccupied.

Tullydraw House at Baxter's Corner, just outside Donaghmore. The television aerial and car would suggest the 1960s.

Mr David Brown, who with his twin brother, Robert, managed the Donaghmore soap-manufacturing firm.

Brown's soap works, Donaghmore, in the first decade of the twentieth century.

The Brown family relaxing on Tullynure Lake around 1900.

A group of employees of the soap works at the beginning of the twentieth century.

Ballymaclinton was a model of an Irish village, built in Shepherd's Bush in London in 1908 by David Brown and Sons Ltd, as part of the Franco-British Exhibition of that year. The village had its round tower, Celtic cross – based, no doubt, on the one in Donaghmore – Blarney Stone, blacksmith's and shoemaker's shops, post office, jaunting cars and Irish colleens in traditional costume. The purpose of the village, in addition to advertising the firm's products, was to raise funds by donations from visitors for various charities. Three and a half million visitors were reported over the three years that the village was in existence but, as the number was dwindling, the large rent forced its closure in October 1910. McClinton's were represented again, however, at the large British Empire exhibition in Wembley in 1924-25. Here the 'village folk' are gathered outside one of the thatched, white-washed houses of the village at the White City, London, in August 1910.

Norah Gallaher, Kathleen Hicks and ? Routledge pose at the base of the Old Cross in Ballymaclinton.

Norah Gallaher wrote in pencil on the back of this card: 'me when I was 3 with what was supposed to be the smallest pony in the world, "Napper Tandy".'

The blacksmith's shop, Ballymaclinton, at Wembley in 1924.

The Burges family home at Parkanaur. The land on which it stands had originally been granted to Sir Toby Caulfield and purchased by the Burges family in the late eighteenth century. When it was sold again in the 1950s, it was bought by Thomas Doran, a local man, who had made a fortune in America, and he donated it as a centre for the education and training of children with disabilities.

The factory at Castlecaulfield.

Pomeroy House, built by the Lowry family in the late eighteenth century.

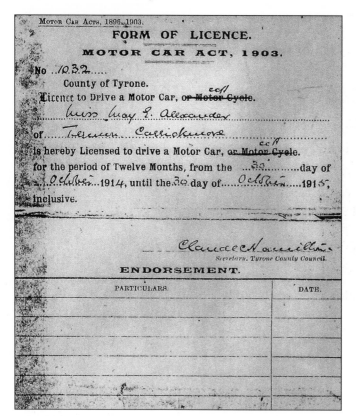

One of the first driving licences around Pomeroy was issued to Miss May E. Alexander in October 1914.

A poultry class in Pomeroy in 1929 with their instructress, Miss Woods, on the left.

A procession makes its way down Main Street, Pomeroy, *en route* to the Mass Garden in Munderadoe, where a special benediction was celebrated in 1932 to mark the Eucharistic Congress in Dublin. A contemporary newspaper report ends: 'The procession was marshalled by Messrs J. Donnelly, P. Gilmartin, P. Fox, J.F. McGurk, J. Beggs, J. Grimes, G. McGuone, J.F. Dynes, J. Quinn, D. Hughes, J. Nugent, P. Begley, P. Quinn, J. Corrigan, M. McKernan, J. Kilpatrick, D. McNally, C. O'Neill, J.F. Grimes JP, P. McAleer, T. Lavery, H. Donnelly, J. Anderson PET, P. Murphy, F. Hagan, B. Harte, L. Brogan, H.M. O'Hare, P. Kelly and T. Devlin PET.'

The scene in the Mass Garden during benediction, with Munderadoe Hall in the background.

Mr Michael McKernan of Pomeroy with pony and trap during the 1930s.

John McGorry outside his shop, which has long since disappeared, in Main Street, Pomeroy.

James Kilpatrick at the door of his shop in Main Street, Pomeroy, in the 1940s. A contemporary advertisement for the shop reads: 'Motor and cycle repairs, petrol, oil and air service. Motor, tractor and cycle tyres, New Hudson, Hopper, Elswick, Rudge, Raleigh and Robin Hood cycles. Ever Ready, Ecko, Cosser and Marconi radios. Radio and car batteries supplied and charged. Aladdin and Tilley lamps, sales and service. Harper's and Skerry boots and shoes. Grocery, hardware and feeding stuffs. Electrical supplies and repairs. Oils, paints and distempers. Motor insurance.'

Bigley's shop at Upper Main Street, Pomeroy. Patrick Begley, as it is now spelt, was grandfather of the country and western singer, Philomena Begley.

Miss Sarah McElhatton – or 'Sally the Bottle' as she was better known – was a familiar sight in the Pomeroy area in the first half of the twentieth century. She dressed alike in all seasons with a long garment from chin to toes, held in place with large safety-pins and a thick, leather belt with a large, silvery buckle around her waist. Her headgear was a man's hat – for a while it was a policeman's cap without a peak – and on her feet she wore a pair of hob-nailed boots. She smoked a large pipe with a silvery lid. Across her right shoulder she carried a sack filled with bottles, hence her name. She held the sack in her left hand and in her right she carried a blackthorn stick with a silver tip as an aid to walking or to administer a swift and sore rebuke to any 'damned scabs', as she called them, who taunted her and were foolish enough to remain within arm's reach. On her left arm she carried a large tin can with an assortment of articles, such as spools of cotton thread, needles and pins. Although she had her own house in the townland of Corrycroar, she travelled the roads every day – taking a different route each day like a door-to-door salesman. On her outward journey she would leave two bottles at each house, one for milk and one for buttermilk, which she used to feed the many dogs and cats which she kept around her house. She would stop in each house for a mug of tea, well-buttered, home-made bread, a smoke of her pipe and a chat. On her return journey in the evening she would collect the filled bottles and reward the householder with something from the can on her left arm. She attended every funeral in the area, regardless of the creed or class of the deceased. Many wondered whether her charity would be remembered and acknowledged when she herself passed away. As it turned out, her funeral in the mid-1950s was one of the largest ever seen in the village. Her passing marked the end of an era.

Arthur Roth, seen here riding in the 1950s, has strong links with Pomeroy. Born in New York after the death of his German father, he was orphaned at the age of five when his mother, who came from the Pomeroy area, died. He spent the next few years in various orphanages in the United States until, at the age of twelve, his aunt, Mrs Carrie Lagan of Pomeroy, brought him to Ireland where he finished his schooling. He worked at different jobs, and even had a spell in the Irish Army, before returning to New York in the late 1940s. There he worked by day to pay his way through night-school and eventually graduated with an honours degree in English. He became a full-time writer and before his death had several novels published. His first, *A Terrible Beauty*, set in a fictitious Irish village – a thinly-disguised Pomeroy – and peopled with thinly-disguised Pomeroy characters, became a best-seller. The film rights of it were acquired by Robert Mitchum, the Hollywood actor and a personal friend of Roth. Mitchum directed the film and starred in it when it was made in Ireland in 1958. It had a strong cast of Hollywood, English and Irish actors, and it marked the screen debut of the Irish actor, Richard Harris, who was destined to become one of the cinema greats.

At work on a farm near Pomeroy during the Second World War.

A peaceful scene in the village of Benburb in the late 1940s.

The Old Castle at Benburb.

Standing to attention at the ceremonies to mark the opening of the Servite Priory, at Benburb in 1949. Third from left is the Irish Prime Minister, John A. Costello, with his aide-de-camp on his left. Second from left is Eamon De Valera, then leader of Fianna Fáil and later President of Ireland. On the left is Frank Aiken, who was a cabinet minister in several Fianna Fáil governments.

Benburb church in the 1940s.

Lineside, Coalisland, with two swans in the Canal basin, in the 1940s.

Mamie's Corner, Coalisland, in the 1940s.

Factory Row in Moygashel in the early 1900s. Moygashel became internationally renowned for its Irish linen textiles which were exported all over the world.

Roxborough Castle at Moy in the early part of this century.

Moy Fair was one of the leading horse fairs in Europe in the first half of this century, but the decline in the commercial use of the horse brought about its demise.

Simple mechanized farming near Edendork between the wars.

A threshing scene on Fay Daly's farm at Crubna, Eglish, in 1928. The thresher was owned by Jack Stafford.

St John's Catholic church at Galbally.

St Brigid's Catholic church, Laghey.

Three
Sport

Dungannon Cricket Club, winners of Qualifying League, Section F, 1956. From left to right, back row: E. McNamee (treasurer), R. McNamee, R. Brown, E. Hodgett, P. Homan, F. Ryan, D. Burrowes, D. Nesbit (secretary). Front row: W. Duff, J. Kerr, T. Milligan, R. Nixon, J. Crook. The club was formed in 1865, lapsed during the First World War and was re-formed in 1948.

Dungannon Cricket Club, winners of the Waring Cup, 1970. From left to right, back row: F. Clark, D. Johnston, J. Irwin, A. Buchanan, J. Chambers, B. Connolly. Front row: W. Adrain, P. Orr, C. Rea, D. Costelloe, D. Burrowes.

Philip Orr batting. On the left is Everton Mattis, the West Indies test player.

The Irish Provincial Towns and Ulster Junior Cups team of Dungannon Rugby Football Club, 1911/12. Inset: B. Kelly, H. McManus. From left to right, back row: E. Kelly, R.J. Grant, J.J. Mills, S.M. Cross, R. Stevenson Esq. (president), R.W. Bingham Esq., A.R. McKinley, L. Richardson, H. Hamilton, W. Brown. Middle row: H.G. Benson, J. Clugson, S. Little, J.O. Hamilton (captain), J. Brown, J. Jackson, G. Gallagher, H.A. Beatty. Front row: J. Gillespie, F. Gill. The club was formed in 1873.

Dungannon RFC, winners of the Provincial Towns' Cup, 1947/48. From left to right, back row: P.A. Bookless, P.M. Evans, J.H. Crooks, S.J. Courtney, A. Sinclair, D.J. Hamill. Middle row: M.A.N. Gilpin, V.R. Johnston, S.R.L. Millar (vice-captain), W.N. Maitland (captain), J.F. Jackson, J.S. Farnham, J.H. Smith. Front row: A.W. Browne, E.W. Ferry.

Dungannon RFC, winners of the Ulster Senior Challenge Cup, Ulster Senior League and Kyle Cup, 1967/68. From left to right, back row: W.E. Shiells, W.K. Armstrong, J.A. Jackson, E.H. Stafford, T.D. Corr, S.V. Patterson, J.B. Nelson, B.T. George, S.N. Armstrong, W.G.H. Wright. Middle row: T.J. Buckley, J.C. Davidson, D.A. Crawford (captain), R.H.B. Mills (president), J.J. Redpath, J.W. McKee, J.D. McKeen. Front row: W. Harper, T.A. Ellison, W.J. Davidson, G.C. Spotswood.

John Robinson McDonald JP, first captain of Dungannon Golf Club, 1890/91.

Dungannon Cowdy Cup-winning team of 1923. From left to right, seated: Samuel Wilson, W.J. Neill, W.J. Thompson. Standing: Jack Wilson, Major T.C.H. Dickson, W.J. Robinson, Tom Wilson, W.J. Hunter.

Dungannon Cowdy Cup-winning team of 1970. From left to right, standing: Jennifer Eitel, -?-, Mary Burrowes, Margaret Simpson, Pat Connolly. Seated: Esme Browne, Mary Stirling, Rosemary Dickson, Muriel Virtue.

Dungannon Craobh Ruadh Gaelic football team, 1911. The team was in existence from 1907 to 1919.

Stewartstown Harps Gaelic football team, 1916. From left to right, back row: John Rushe, Paddy Quinn, Dan Doey, John Devlin, Paddy Mulgrew, Johnny Tohill, Joe Smith. Middle row: Joe Canavan, Barney Herron, Frank Clarke, Peter Corr. Front row: 'Fashy' Davidson, Paddy Donnelly, Johnny Morrison, Paddy Clarke, Geordie Rodgers. The Harps were first registered as a club in 1916, lapsed in 1918, and were re-formed in1923.

Stewartstown Harps GFC, 1923. Left to right, back row: Seamus Lynch, J. Donnelly, Eddie Ryan, Willie John Laverty, Paddy Devlin. Middle row: Micky McArdle, Francie Fee, Peter Mulgrew. Front row: Francis Tohill, Tom McGrath, 'Fashy' Davidson, John O'Neill, Paddy Rea.

Moy Tír na nÓg GFC, Tyrone senior champions, 1920. From left to right, back row: E. Conroy (treasurer), E. Finn, D.J. Hegarty, H.P. McSorley, T.P. Hegarty, T. McVeigh, P. Tohall (chairman), J.P. Byrne (secretary). Middle row: R.M. Clancy, F. O'Neill, C. Byrne, J.Byrne, J. McManus, T.J. Twomey, J. Campbell, P. Curran. The club was established in 1908.

Mountjoy Emmett's GFC in 1922. From left to right, back row: Pat Gillis, Arthur Quinn, James Dorman, Bernard Kilpatrick, Joe Corr, John Canavan. Top right-hand corner: Eddie Forbes. Middle row: Peter Dorman, Charlie Bigger, Frank Clarke (captain), James Quinn, Dan McSloy. Front: Peter Quinn. The club was officially established in 1925.

Clonoe O'Rahilly's GFC in 1923. From left to right, back row: Joe O'Neill, Peter Corr, Mick O'Neill, James P. Donnelly, Jody O'Hanlon, Pat O'Neill. Front row: Terence McGrath, John Joe Dorman, Hugh O'Neill, Barney O'Neill, Joe Devlin, John Cushnahan.

Donaghmore Éire Óg GFC, county champions and first holders of the O'Neill Cup in 1927. From left to right, back row: Barney McGlade, James McCourt, Frank Leonard, Canon O'Neill PP, Tommy McCausland, Mick Loughran, Jim Morgan. Middle row: Tommy Comac, Tommy Gallagher, Johnny McCullagh, Jim McLernon, Tommy Murphy, Billy Keogh, Paddy McLernon, Jimmy Quinn, Mick Daly, Mick O'Neill. Front row: Mick Loughran, Harry Campbell, Peter McLernon, Jimmy McCourt. The club was founded in 1903.

Pomeroy Plunketts' GFC in 1932. Included are: P. McCourt, Leo McMenemy, Pat Paul Kelly, Vincey Beggs, Packie Begley, Charlie McDonald, Pat McConnell, Hugh Michael O'Hare, John Hagan, Packie Corrigan, Mick Gilmartin. The club was formed in the 1916/17 season.

Brackaville Owen Roe's GFC in 1938. From left to right, back row: Tom Carberry, Jimmy Graham, Seamus Toner, Kevin Doherty, Seamus Badley, Pat Quinn, Peter Toner, Barney Corey, Peter Toner Snr, Peter Toner Jnr. Front row: H.P. McNally, Jim McCaughery, Willie McIlvenna, Charlie McNally, Paddy Early, Dixie Morgan, Packie Devlin, John Joe Symington. The club was established in 1938.

Derrytresk Fir-an-Chnuic GFC in 1940. From left to right, back row: Barney Teggart, Johnny McCann, Mick Ryan, Alec Begley, James Burns, A.P. McGrath, Peter McGrath, Pat O'Neill. Front Row: Arthur Campbell, Owenie Campbell, Peter Fitzgerald, James O'Neill, John Joe Campbell. The club was first established in 1905.

Derrylaughan Kevin Barry's GFC in the late 1940s. From left to right, back row: Joe Corr, Francie Teggart, James McAliskey, Jimmy Teggart, Arthur McGuinness, Sean McCann, Gerry McAliskey, Paddy Quinn. Front row: Mick Quinn, James Quinn, Francie McCann, Paddy McCann, Paddy McCann, Micky Dorman, John Robinson. The present club was formed in 1944.

Thomas Clarke's GFC, Dungannon, county champions in 1947. From left to right, back row: J. Casey, D. Kelly, Johnny Harte, P. Mullen, J.Campbell, J. Quinn, P.K. O'Neill, Joe Harte, A. Small, D. Begley, S. Mallon, V. Fox. Front row: F. Fee, P. Fox, T. Campbell, I. Jones, T. Corrigan, J. Morrison, J. Skeffington, J. Rafferty. The present club was established in 1917.

Eglish St Patrick's GFC in the late 1960s. The club was established in 1956.

Galbally Pearses' GFC in the mid-1950s. From left to right, back row: Pat Tally, Aeneas Quinn, Paddy Arthurs, Pat McKenna, Austin Corr, John McKeown, Joe Cassidy, James Maguire. Front row: Packie Nugent, Tom Quinn, Pat Hagan, Henry Murphy, Frank McKenna, John Quinn, Pat Rafferty. The club was registered in August 1949.

Rock St Patrick's GFC in the late 1950s. From left to right, back row: Dermot McLernon, James Kolbohm, Paddy Mullan, Micky Sloane, B.J. Skeffington, Felix McGeough, Paddy Cush, Johnny Lawn, Peter McLernon, M.J. McCourt. Front row: J.J. Corr, Eugene Quinn, Patsy Heaney, Malachy Campbell, Brian Morris. The present club was re-formed in 1977.

Killyman St Mary's GFC, which made its debut in April 1964. From left to right, back row: Peter McGahan, Des McGahan, Jimmy McGahan, Brian Hughes, Peadar McGahan, Gerard McVeigh, Jack McGahan, Johnny McGahan, Dan McAlinden, Brendan McGahan, John Joe McVeigh, Patsy McVeigh, Brian O'Neill, Gabriel Farrell, John Charlie Hughes, Tommy Muldoon. Front row: Michael Donnelly, John Hughes, Eamon Quinn, Dermot McGahan, Frank McAlinden, Sean Farmer, Tommy Lavery, John Kernaghan, Gary McGahan, Tommy McGahan.

The committee and workers responsible for constructing Plunkett Park, Pomeroy, in 1948. From left to right, back row: Bob Devlin, Johnny Kerr, Joe Begley, Mickey Murphy, Anthony Nugent, Dan Cush. Fourth row: Hugh Corrigan, George McGuone, Johnny McNally, Brian Mullen (Murnells). Third row: Tom Grimes, Barney McNally, Packie Murphy, Liam Donnelly, Sean Kilpatrick, Vincent McCallan, Tommy Devlin. Second row: Pete Begley, James Corrigan, Dermot Corrigan, Mickey McKernan, Brendan Casey, Paddy Cunningham, Hughie Rafferty. Front row, seated: Johnny Anderson PT, Leo Donnelly, Johnny McGeary, Paddy Conlon, Charlie Rafferty, Al Beggs, Pat Cush. Kneeling at front: Petesy Nugent, Patsy Begley, Brian Quinn.

Dungannon Swifts Football Club, 1949/50. From left to right, back row: Jackie McCarthy, Bob Talbot, Billy McKee, Joe Meldrum, Freddie Neill, Ernest Murphy, Maurice Graham. Front row: Alfie Burnett, Victor Flack, Sammy Lawson, David Flack, Tommy Elliott, Noel McKennan, John Martin.

Dungannon Swifts FC in the late 1960s. From left to right, back row: B. Parker, B. Lawson, J. Rafferty, G. Clarke, D. Shannon. Front row: W. Steenson, I. Scott, W. Jennings, G. Scott (captain), R. Todd, R. McIlwaine.

The Dungannon Swifts Football Club's first dressing-rooms with a good luck emblem above the door.

Loughgall Football Club in 1935. From left to right, back row: Ted Calvin, Bill Bartholomew, Harold Proctor, Bill Vallelly, Richard Grafton, Eddie McVeigh. Middle row: Harry Currie, Horace Moore, Davy Calvin, Sam Calvin, Davy Guy, Jimmy Robinson. Front row: George McAllister, Thomas Henry Currie, Bobby Herron. Soccer in Loughgall dates back to the late nineteenth century.

Dungannon Eoghan Ruadh hurling team in 1950. From left to right, back row: Harry McBride, Frank Cavanagh, Johnny Harte, Paul Stewart, Les Statham, Joey Harte, Mick Haughey. Middle row: Pat O'Donnell, John O'Donnell. Front row: Paddy McCrea, Billy Ritchie, Barney McBride, Teddy Devlin, Mick McHugh, Billy Ross.

St Ita's camogie team, Dungannon, winners of the County Championship. From left to right, back row: M. Devlin, F. Murphy, T. Cullen, C. McCaul, M. Rafferty, E. Donaghy, M. Donnelly. Front row: M. Kelly, M. Hillen, M. Donaghy, I. Conlan, K. Devlin, M. McCaul. Hurling and camogie have been promoted in Dungannon since the 1930s.

Eglish St Teresa's Camogie Club, formed in 1966 and regular winners of the County Championship from then onwards. This is the 1969 team with the trophy. From left to right, back row: Rose McCaul, Bernadette Daly, Angela Hamill, Anthony Donaghy, Dympna Hamill, Maire Farley, Phil Hamill. Front row: Maire Regan, Margaret Donaghy, Cassie McCaul, Mary Donaghy, Maureen Daly, Margaret Donaghy.

Derrylaughan St Patrick's camogie team in 1982.

Clonoe St Ann's camogie team in 1969. From left to right, back row: Mary Ann Hanna, Bernadette McKee, Sylvia Canavan, Marietta Canavan, Philomena O'Neill, Josie Scullion, Mairead McStravock, Deirdre Duffin, Cathie Donnelly. Front row: Patricia Canavan, Ann Skeffington, Cecelia Devlin, Kathy Fee, Dolores Canavan, Monica Devlin, Annette McAliskey.

Kingsisland St Colmcille's camogie team around 1980. From left to right, back row: Deirdre Fitzgerald, Rosaleen Hanna, Margaret Hanna, Martina Fitzgerald, Margaret Daly, Jackie McCann, Sheila Fitzgerald, Sheila Campbell, Peggy O'Neill, Maureen Campbell, Edna O'Neill, Bridget Fitzgerald, Pauline Fitzgerald. Front row: Eilish Hanna, Kathleen Hanna, Patricia Canavan, Marie Ryan, Maura Fitzgerald, Martina Daly, Angeline O'Neill.

The Granville Harriermen, 1951.

A well-earned rest for huntsmen and hounds, 1951.

Four

Bands

Micky McNally leads Pomeroy Accordion Band along Ann Street, Dungannon, in the early 1950s. Charlie O'Neill, Mick Fox and Joe Begley form the front rank of the band, while further back John Loughran, Micky Harte and Tony Corr may be seen. Looking on from the right is well known Dungannon resident, P.G. McQuaid.

Augharan LOL and Pipe Band in 1923. From left to right, front row: Bob McIvor, Thomas Wilkinson, Bob McAteer, Fred Davidson, George Moffett, George Davidson, George Wilson, R.J. Davis, Willie Reid, George Brown. Second row: Bob Brown, David Moore, Tommy Burrows, Sandy Hewitt, Whiteside Burrows, Bob Williamson, Joe Seawright (Worshipful Master), James Beggs, Thomas Montgomery, John Proctor, Thomas Seawright, Thomas Beggs, Sam Somerville. Third row: Willie John Reid, John Greaves, James Burrows, Sam McIvor, Joe Davidson, Leslie Hewitt (Pipe Major), Richard Wilkinson, Jim Burrows, Andy Harris, Sam Davidson, Robert J. Burrows, George Davis, George Davidson. Back row: James Wilkinson, Wilson Beggs, Jim Ford, W. Hewitt, T. Greaves.

Tullyallen Pipe Band parade along Irish Street and Ann Street, Dungannon, on St Patrick's Day 1951.

Dungannon AOH Band on 16 March 1963. From left to right, back row: John Foley, Paddy Kerr, Bertie Farrell, Brendan Foley, Benny Creggan, Billy Hughes, Terry Foley, John Mullan, Jerry McCabe, Jimmy Foley, Paddy Rea, Patsy Gallagher. Front row: Colm Hamilton, Oliver Gallagher, Joe Regan, Paddy Donnelly, Jackie Hazley, Mick McHugh, Peter Regan.

The Craobh Ruadh Céilí Band supplies the music during a Dungannon GAA Céilí.

Dungannon INF Silver Band parades in the Market Square in the 1950s. The names on the buildings in the background, 'The Cosmo Café' and 'Fred W. Robinson', have long since gone.

The Comac Brothers' Céilí Band from Donaghmore, with Miss Vera Devlin on the piano, was much in demand during the 1940s and 1950s.

The Owen Roe AOH Flute Band from Stewartstown in the first half of the twentieth century.

Donaghmore AOH Band assembles outside the old hall (now Rotharlann) in the late 1920s. Drummers at the front, left to right are: Pat Loughran, John Quinn and Joe Haughey. Another Mr Haughey is on the big drum and James Hetherington plays the triangle. Among those looking on, from left to right, are: Brian McCluskey, Paddy McCooey, Johnny McCullagh, William Lynch, Joe Donnelly, James McCourt, Frank Leonard, Johnny Hetherington and Peter Skeffington.

Pomeroy Accordion Band marches through Carrickmore in the 1950s.

Five

Schools

Moy No. 2 Elementary National School in 1909.

Pupils at a drawing lesson, Moy No. 2 Elementary National School, 1909.

Girls at a cookery lesson, Moy No. 2 Elementary National School, 1909.

Pupils at drill, Moy No. 2 Elementary National School, 1909.

Kingsisland Primary School in around 1900.

Royal School, Dungannon, 1st XI in 1901. From left to right, back row: M.K. Acheson, R.W. Bingham Esq., D. Smith, H.S. Fergus. Middle row: J.P. Wilson, R.F. Kennedy, C.H. Burgess, C.E.P. Browne, R.F. Harper. Front row: P. Ross-Todd, C. Thompson, W. Porter.

Clintyclay Primary School in 1909.

Tullysaran Primary School, 1911. From left to right, back row: Mr J. Coyle, A. Coyle, L. McVeigh, H. Hughes, M. McParland, C. McAnallen, L. Britt, E. Britt, M. McDonald, M. Conlon, Miss M. Coyle. Second row: P. McGahan, O. McParland, M. Hughes, M. Sherry, S. Smyth, A. McKenna, S.A. McAnallen, J. McVeigh, P.J. Hughes, G. McAnallen, F. McGahan, J. Smyth, P. Conlon. Third row: L. McGirr, J. Smyth, E. McDonald, B. Conlon, L. McGirr, P. McKenna, J. McKenna, M. Hughes, M. Joyce, B. Mallon, M. Kernan, E. McAnallen. Fourth row: P. McVeigh, N. McVeigh, E. McGahan, P. Donnelly, D. Donnelly, J. Kernan, T. Hughes, Joe Hughes, Jim Hughes, P. Hughes.

St Patrick's Primary School, Dungannon, in the early years of the twentieth century.

Edendork chapel and primary school around 1900. The school was on the opposite side of the road from today's building, beside the chapel. The pupils, accompanied by the schoolmaster wearing his hat, have lined the wall and roadside, as if waiting for something to come along. The poster on the gatepost, advertising a show, may have something to do with it.

PE class at the Royal School, Dungannon, in 1920 under Drill Sergeant Bould. From left to right, back row: H.R. Browne, -?-. Third row: F.H. Ferris, -?-, J.G. Grogan, -?-. Second row: J. Law, -?-, J.T. Rea, M. Wilson, J. McMaster, -?-, -?-. Front row: W. Johnston, -?-, A.G.C. Ffolliott, T.L. Bamford, C.J. Irwin, H.D. Watson, T.S. Macoun, N.E.G. Sinton.

Roan Primary School juniors in May 1923.

Tullysaran Primary School, 1921. From left to right, back row: James Corrigan, Joe Sheridan, -?-, Harry Hughes, Annie White, M.E. Donnelly, Jim McKee, J. McNamara, John Hughes, -?-, Mr James Coyle. Third row: Miss M. Coyle, John McVeigh, Alice McKenna, R. McCartan, Hugh Sheridan, Mary Passmore, T. McGirr, Kitty Corrigan, M. Ann Hughes, L. Hughes, Maggie McGahan. Second row: James Passmore, Paddy Donnelly, Mary Corrigan, Dan McGurk, Annie Kernan, W.J. McGahan, James Hughes, John Hughes, Jim Morgan, James McGahan. Front row: Nancy Passmore, Kitty McGurk, Mary McGahan, Maggie Kerr, Francie Donnelly, Joe White, Jerry McVeigh, Henry Corrigan.

Slatequarry Primary School in the 1920s, with teacher, Mr. T Devlin.

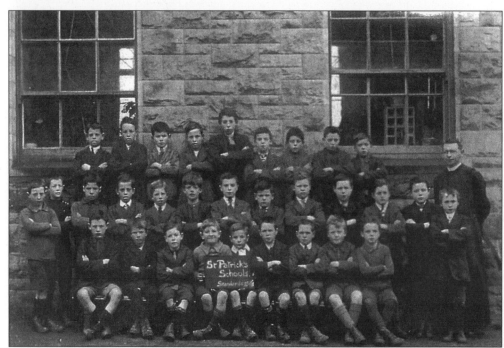

St Patrick's Primary School, Dungannon, in the 1920s. From left to right, back row: M. Harte, ? McCaughey, J. Campbell, J. Mallon, Paddy Vincent, ? Murphy, ? Kelly, Chris McFall. J. McQuaid. Second row: J. Bloomer, Pat McGarvey, ? Hughes, J. Quinn, Joe Rice, -?-, Charlie Woods, W. Wilson, ? Clarke, Jimmy Richards. Front row: ? Barker, ? Morrison, ? Ferran, Tommy Cavanagh.

Aughnagar Primary School in 1925.

Tullyroan Primary School (senior class) in 1925, with Mr Ben Allen, principal. From left to right, back row: Alice Lawson, Lizzie Reid, Martha Reid, Nan Gilpin, Rachel Richardson, Mabel Lawson, Ena Reid, Carrie Hayes, Ruby Irwin. Third row: Albert Murray, Jerry Wright, John Foy, George Gilpin, Jim Richardson, Norman Gilpin, Henry Murray, Joe Stevenson, George Thompson. Second row: Evelyn Davidson, Gladys Matchett, ? Downey, Hilda Wilson, Hannah Elliott, Meta Gilpin, Edie Reid, Gertie Matchett, Isabel Gilpin, Jim Gilpin. Front row: Ruby Lawson, Thomas William Irwin, Willie Reid, John Cahoon, Jim Murray, Ben Mullen, Norman Davidson, Edwin Hayes.

Cranlome Primary School in the 1920s.

Kingsisland Primary School in the mid 1920s. From left to right, back row: Willie Joe Heaney, Arthur Campbell, Johnny Taggart, Joe Timlin, John P. Foster, Barney O'Neill, John J. Campbell, Matt Devlin, John McCabe. Third row: Miss Morrisey, Pat McAliskey, Bridget McAliskey, Mary T. McCann, Kathleen Foster, Rose Fitzgerald, Rose Devlin, Catherine McAliskey, John McLaughlin, Mrs Cullen. Second row: Joe Paddy McCabe, Emma Joanna McCabe, Teresa Quinn, Mary Ellen McCabe, Bella Timlin, John F. McGrath, James McAliskey, Jim Fitzgerald. Front row: Francis Taggart, Hugh Herron, James Taggart, Mollie McCann, Peggy Magennis, Mary Magennis, Sarah Fitzgerald, Mary Ellen Hanna, Teresa Hanna, Sarah Ann Hanna.

Brocagh Primary School in the 1930s.

Cavanbellaghy Primary School in 1928. From left to right, back row: Mrs Mills, Charlie Williamson, Sam Vogan, John Campbell, John Nesbitt, George Prentice, John Henderson, John Duffy. Third row: Doris McKinney, Archie Campbell, John Wilson, Doris Millar, Francis Gillespie, Hannah Vogan, Maimie Foster, Maggie Mann, Willie Williamson, Tommy Williamson, Sam Vogan. Second row: ? Bridges, George Posnett, Willie Anderson, Tillie Wilson, May Gillespie, Ann Gillespie, -?-. Front row: Betty Dougan, ? Foster, Willie Mann, ? Bridges, Eric Nesbitt, Jackie Posnett. Some of these pupils transferred to Drumsallen School when it opened in 1931.

Clintyclay Primary School in 1931.

Killeshill Primary School in 1936.

Donaghey Primary School in 1935. From left to right, back row: Mrs Baird, George Harkness, Thomas Cuddy, John Bowden, Sam Hagen, David Forrest, Joe Ferguson, Harry McKane, John Millar, John Anderson, Albert Ferguson, George Forrest, Rowley Kells, Robert J. Bell, Joe Millar, Isaac Nethercote, Hugh Ferguson, Sandy Forrest, Tommy Burns, Cecil Bell, Bertie Millar, Jack McKane, Master Baird (principal). Middle row: Austin Anderson, Willie Hagen, Peggy Hagen, Annie Cuddy, Florence Millar, Jean Hagen, May Sloan, Jean Millar, Lily Nethercote, Lizzie Thompson, Ethel Parke, Olive Graham, Cissie Lyttle, Mabel Wilson, Ella Sloan, Ina Patton, Jim Pickering, Cecil Campbell, Bobby Nethercote, William J. Cuddy. Front row: -?-, Sam Cuddy, -?-, Maxie Wilson, Ernie Anderson, Stanley Anderson, Harry Forrest, Mary Parke, Muriel Nethercote, Emily Wilson, May Wallace, Peggy Forrest, Muriel Bowden, Lily Boyd Betty Wilson, Florence Millar, Maggie Ferguson, Lily Glass, Willie Ferguson, Wesley Wallace. George Forrest, twelfth from left in the back row, was later Westminster MP for the constituency.

Tamnamore Primary School, 1936. From left to right, back row: John Farrell, William Robert Hughes, Tommy Beattie, Jim Blevins, Leslie Blair, Melvyn Cranston, Bertie Kelso, Albert Blair, Bill Robinson. Middle row: Elsie Blair, Florrie Riddell, Lucy Currie, Dot Willis, May Blair, Jeannie Currie, Cissie Farrell, Nellie Beattie, Jean Hamilton, Bessie Henderson, Doreen Hazelton, Olive Kelso. Front row: Dorothy Chapman, Molly Duke, Jean Henderson, Eileen Graham, Master William Steele, Jean McComb, Violet Blair, Rachel Hughes, Mabel McComb.

St Patrick's Boys' Academy, Dungannon, in the mid 1930s.

St Patrick's Girls' Academy, Dungannon, in 1937.

Castlecaulfield Primary School No. 1 in 1938. From left to right, back row: David Scott, Bertie Henderson, Albert Crawford, Fred Kelly, Wesley Hall, Roy Tener, Richard Bartley, Robert McMahon, Jack Davidson. Third row: May Truesdale, Joan Graham, Bertha Dougal, Mervyn Crawford, Tommy Hanna, Leslie McIlree, Albert Wilson, ShirleyYoung, Betty Kelly, Willie Davidson, Isobel Hinchy, Florrie Meneely, Iona Graham, Mary Hanna, Margaret Rankin. Second row: -?-, Rita Scott, Beatrice Rowan, Wesley Rowan, Leslie Wilson, Robert Grimes, Jim Davidson, Kenneth Campbell, Malcolm Campbell, Freddie Phillips, Edith Reid. Front row: Margaret Ferguson, -?-, Kathleen Bartley, Brenda Kelly, Maud Kelly, Dorothy Dougal, Jean Dougal.

Kingsisland Primary School in the mid-1940s, with Mr Felix Morgan, the principal.

Roan Primary School in the 1940s.

100

Newmills Primary School around 1940. From left to right, back row: Thomas Patterson, Joseph Brodison, William Stewart, Ernie Moffett, James Baird, Alan Moffett, Robert Stewart. Fourth row: Miss Weir (teacher), Ruby Boyd, Molly Hardy, Annie Brodison, Florrie Patterson, Norah Wright, Violet Patterson, Winnie Moffett, Emily Stewart, Gladys Gallagher, Mina Badger, Minnie Brodison. Third row: Thomas Badger, Lottie Brodison, Maggie Brodison, Olive Wright, Violet Badger, Mary Badger, Rebecca Todd, Molly Beggs, Kathleen Boyd, Lizzie Stewart, Violet Wylie, Kitchener Patterson, Joe Hardy, Master Wright. Second row: Robert Todd, Robert Boyd, Bobby Beggs, Sam Brodison, May Boyd, Maggie Stewart. Front row: Percy Moffett, Norman Moffett, Andy Baird, Minnie Baird, Willie Brodison, Davy Stewart, Wilfred Wright, Lorna Boyd, Joan Wright, May Patterson, Eric Montgomery, Joe Baird, William Baird.

Kilnaslee Primary School in the 1940s. From left to right, back row: teacher, Ronnie Moore, Eric Watt, Hilda McMinn, Mervyn McMinn, David Henderson, Raymond Moore. Front row: William Gilkinson, Anna Gilkinson, Joy Moore, Pearl Gilkinson, Jean McMinn, Greta Watt, Julia Gilkinson, Helen McMinn, Roy Welton. Seated at the front: William McIvor.

Killylevin Primary School in the 1940s.

St Mary's Girls' Primary School, Pomeroy, around 1950. From left to right, back row: Paddy Harding, Ellen Simpson, Anna Anderson, Maria Mallaghan, Sue Quinn, Mary Rafferty, Vera Keenan, Marie McArdle, Ita Rafftery. Second row: Kate Daly, Bridget McDonagh, Olive Devlin, Kathleen Stewart, Anne Casey, Winnie McDonagh, Margaret Conlon, Seraphine Conway, Teresa Conlon, Annette Begley, Rosaleen Casey, Mary Begley. Front row: Marie Stewart, Carmel Morgan, Claire Fulton, Patricia McDonald, Mamie McKernan, Kathleen McGinn, Vera Nugent, Mary Quinn, Eileen Murphy, Ann Donnelly, Breige McAloon, Sheila Mary Boyle, Bridie McArdle, Cliodhna McAleer, Bridie Devlin, Gloria Creggan.

Tamnamore Primary School in 1952.

Kerrib Primary School in 1948. From left to right, back row: Brian McGeough, Peter Daly, Simon Daly, Peggy Donnelly, Teresa McVeigh, Rosie McVeigh, Margaret McVeigh, Brigid McVeigh, Mary Quinn, Packie Corrigan, Sylvie Quinn, Pat Daly, Pat Quinn, Winston Burnside, Patrick McGeary. Third row: Master Robert Troddyn (the principal), Sean McVeigh, Patsy Hagan (brother of the author), Ivan Burnside, Aeneas Quinn, Barbara Nixon, Mary Donnelly, Lettie Quinn, Eileen McGeary, Betty Robinson, Teresa Quinn. Second row: Mina Bell, Eileen McVeigh, Billy Hayes, Jim Quinn, Bridget Ann Corrigan, Brian McGarrity, Felix Hagan (the author), John Moore, Thomas Brian Quinn, Maggie Clarke, Eileen Hayden, Dominic Hayden, John Quinn, Jimmy Quinn. Front row (seated): Columba Hagan (brother of author), William Moore, John Coyle, Josie Quinn, Philomena Donnelly, Doreen Moore, Georgina Moore, Jim Beggs, John McGeary, Colm McGeary, Mary Coyle, Briany Clarke.

Lisfearty Primary School in 1949. From left to right, back row: Master Tom Porter, Ivan Paisley, Doreen Clarke, Marcella Alexander, Gladys Williamson, Myrtle Knox, Colin Campbell. Fourth row: John Moore, Gerald Pike, Emma Dickson, Peggy Williamson, Fladda Williamson, Vera Armstrong, Bessie Dickson, Mrs. Simpson, Pearl Alexander. Third row: Mona McVeigh, Dorothy Beattie Roland Beattie, Jim Williamson, Mervyn Hall, Iris Pike, Elsa Dickson, Ina Rutherford, Isabel Clarke. Second row (seated on chairs): Cecil Knox, Helen Sharkey, Olive Pike, Nancy Sharkey, Bertha Knox, Freddie Williamson, Violet Lamont. Front row (seated on the ground): Kenneth Givan, Alexander Condy, John Stinson.

Killyman Primary School (Junior School) in 1950. From left to right, back row: James Craig, Robert Graham, Frankie Benson, Alex Kennedy, Charlie Williamson, Jackie Douglas, Sam Mullen, Douglas Cardwell, Jackie Williamson, Herbert Wallace. Third row: Miss Crawford, Maureen Fowler, Isobel Fowler, Valerie Griffith, Marjorie Lyons, Yvonne McMullan, Helen Jackson, Norah Bradley, Shirley Johnston, Elizabeth Gamble, Betty Flemming, Pauline Jackson, Mrs. Brown. Second row: David Hazelton, Gloria Williamson, Noeleen McMullan, Valerie Gillespie, Barbara Compton, Ann Kennedy (with Jennifer Murphy), Valda Coulter, Connie Graham, Mildred Jenkinson, Joan Flemming, Ida Benson, Eric Steenson, Ivan Steenson. Front row: Winston Wray, William Jenkinson, Kenny Beattie, George Courtenay, Henry Courtenay, Alan McMullan, John Ruddy, Desmond Steenson, John Graham, John Bradley, Roy Black, Maurice Bradley, Kenneth Bradley.

Killyman Primary School (Middle School), 1950. From left to right, back row: K. Cardwell, D. Wray, J. Gilkinson, B. Wray, B. McMorris, G. Forsythe, D. Graham, J. Fowler, I. Mills. Middle row: Miss Appleby (teacher), D. Wray, D. Green, D. Graham, M. Gallagher, B. McMorris, M. Kennedy, M. Courtney, E. Bradley, M. Graham. Front row: T. Blair, A. Ludlow, G. Thompson, S. Graham, H. Ludlow, H. Courtney, M. Cardwell, A. Gamble, E. Peak, H. Bradley, B. Wallace.

Crosscavanagh Primary School in the late 1940s. From left to right, back row: Paul Quinn, John Henry Hughes, Pat McDonnell, Pat Tally, Hugh Hetherington, Paddy Arthurs, Peter Hoines, Peter Tally, Hughie McVeigh, Patrick Joseph Murphy. Third row: Anthony Kyle, Paddy Hetherington, Francis Skeith, Pat Rafferty, Joe Moore, Terry Kelly, Lena Hoines, Rosie Hoines, Mary Ellen Loughran, Gerard Donnelly, Peter Joe Murphy. Second row: Lizzie Armstrong, Rita Armstrong, Catherine Maria Kelly, Mary Carmel Hackett, Ita McCabe, Rose McVeigh, Patricia Hughes, Brigid Quinn. Front row: Jim Kelly, Roddy McDonnell, Cormac McDonnell, Jim Hetherington, Joe Rafferty, Barney Rafferty. The principal is Master Paddy McGrath.

Tullyallen Primary School, 1951/52.

Drumsallen Primary School in 1950. From left to right, back row: Sam Cornett, Richard Carmichael, Jim Lee, Quentin Bloomer, John Bloomer, Alex Wilson, William Carmichael, Ronnie Lester, Hugh Gillespie, Bill Neville. Third row: Jim Bloomer, Robert Gillespie, Quentin Wilson, David Lester, Jim Cornett, Edward Posnett, Joe Gillespie, Sidney Carmichael, George Mills, Henry Bloomer, Norman Lester, David Gillespie, Mrs Willis. Second row: Freda Allen, Betty Lester, Peggy Riddle, Edith Neville, Lily Miller, Pearl Lee, Florence Anderson, Iris Knipe, Dorothy Gillespie, Rosemary Mills, Florence Mann. Front row: Meredith Quinn, Ronald Gillespie, Ann Lester, Noreen Lester, Audrey Clarke, J. Allen, Hilda Neville, Betty Nesbitt, Joy Allen, Hazel Quinn, Fenton Nesbitt, Joy Whyte, Hazel Knipe, Gladys Thompson, Avril Clarke, Tommy Lester.

Castlecaulfield No. 2 Primary School in the early 1950s.

St Mary's Boys' Primary School (Middle School), Pomeroy, in 1954. From left to right, back row: Gerard Keenan, John Goodfellow, Alan Traynor, Brian Donnelly, Frank Campbell, Dermot McNally, Raymond McIntyre, Oliver Beggs, Kevin Casey. Middle row: Malachy Foster, Jimmy Harding, Plunkett Harte, Joe Hamilton, Pat Kelly, Liam McConnell, Leo McVeigh, Plunkett Begley, Sean Coyle. Front row: Jim Murray, Joe Maguire, Barry Lambe, Plunkett Kennedy.

St Joseph's Convent Grammar School, Donaghmore, which had previously been Donaghmore House, the residence of Revd George Walker and, later, Mr Alexander MacKenzie.

Donaghmore railway station was the point of arrival and departure for generations of young boarders at St Joseph's Convent School, Donaghmore. From left to right: Sheila Kennedy, Paddy Kennedy and Mona Kennedy.

Sister M. Brogan, with the Ashbourne Shield, which St Joseph's Convent Grammar School won in the mid-1950s. Standing are Josie McAvoy and Eithne Quinn, while Eilish Twomey and Elizabeth O'Neill sit on the left and right of their teacher.

Laghey Primary School in 1956. From left to right, back row: J. Connolly, S. Cavanagh, J. Hughes, J. Casey, J. Hughes, P. Hutchinson, P. McVeigh, P. McKearney, D. Kelly, G. McVeigh. Third row: J. Hutchinson, M. Kavanagh, A. Henry, S. Hutchinson, B. McGahan, D. McGahan, M. Kelly. Second row: B. Hughes, P. Farrell, D. Farrell, M. Corr, T. Corr, E. Collins, A. McHugh, B. Coleman, B. Kavanagh, C. Cavanagh, M. Cavanagh, A. Campbell, M. Cassidy, A. Cassidy. Front row: M. McVeigh, G. Farrell, R. Hughes, D. Kelly, K. Hughes, M. Hughes, H. Kavanagh.

Tullyroan Primary School in 1957, with teachers Miss Gertie Wilson (later Mrs Lawson) and Mr George Graham.

Walker Memorial School, Castlecaulfield, in the 1950s with the principal, Mr Ernest McNamee. From left to right, back row: R. Morrison, A. Graham, N. Wilson, W. Lynn, G. Kelly, F. Meneely, A. Lambe, J. Crilly. Middle row: N. Doran, G. Wilson, C. Ferguson, G. Kelly, E. Doherty, J. Dugal, M. Ferguson, W. Kelly, H. Meneely, J. Gray, P. Devlin, Master McNamee. Front row: J. Kirk, J. Boyd, A. Bartley, P. Miller, J.Hinchey, J. Truesdale, M. Kirk, M. Ferguson, S. Dugal, E. Doherty, R. Lindsay, N. Grimes, N. Dugal.

Aughamullan Primary School in the mid-1960s, with the teaching staff, Mr. Jim Cavanagh, Miss Peggy Carr and Mrs Sarah McGrath.

Form E of St Patrick's Boys' Academy, Dungannon, 1954-55. In the back row, from left to right, are: Jim McRory, Eric Slater, Joe McCausland, Tom Cullen, Brendan Sheridan, Brendan Fox, Thomas Campbell, Brian Timlin, John Paddy Mullan, Sean Slater. Middle row: Michael McKenna, Patsy Hagan, Fred Lowe, Willie Quinn, Frank McArdle, Vincent Rodgers, Dan Conway, Pat O'Neill, Pat Hunter, John Skelton. Front row: Jim Long, Charlie McCaul, Tony Quinn, John Duffin, Clement Vaughan, Jody O'Neill, Sean Cavanagh, Thomas Kelly, Tommy McConville, Jim Brendan O'Neill.

Ballytrea Primary School in 1959. From left to right, back row: Mrs. Burrowes, Norman Kennedy, Tom Ferguson, Freddie Ferguson, Billy McVitty, William McKeown, Raymond McGahie, Gordon Johnston, Ronnie Farr, Noel Booth, Dessie and Cyril Farr (twins), Miss Badger (later Mrs Bell). Third row: Hazel Spiers, Anna Kirkpatrick, Florence Shannon, Thelma Jeffers, Barbara Spiers, Nora Mullan, Sandra McGahie, Ray Johnston, Denise McGahie, Hazel Farr, Freda Stewart, Shirley McCrea, Muriel Shannon, Margaret Johnston, Ann McGahie, Enid Hamilton. Second row: Ruth McGahie, Margaret Irwin, Valerie Kirkpatrick, Lorna Jeffers, Daphne Ferguson, Hazel Ferguson, Nita Kennedy, Alberta Murphy, Joyce Mullan, Margaret Rea, Geraldine Jeffers. Front row: Cedric Wilson, Roy McGuckin, Sidney Black, Ian Wilson, Alan Hamilton, Bobby Spiers, Leslie McGucken, William Henry, George Booth, Freddie Johnston, Ralph Booth, Bertie Kirkpatrick, Dennis McGucken, David Booth.

The Royal School in Dungannon, showing the old entrance gates.

The unfurling ceremony of the John Nicholson statue in the Royal School grounds in 1960. Nicholson, an ex-pupil of the Royal School, had risen to the rank of Brigadier-General when he was killed on breaching the Kashmir Gate at Delhi. Earl Mountbatten is flanked here by the headmaster, Archibald de Gruchy Gaudin, and head boy, Desmond Scott.

The rounded façade of St Patrick's Secondary Intermediate School, to run parallel with the road, drew much favourable comment when the school was built in the early 1960s.

The original staff of St Patrick's Secondary Intermediate Girls' School in Dungannon. They were: Sister M. Gabrielle, Mrs J. McGartland, Mrs N. Cassidy, Mrs M. Woods, Mrs C. Conroy, Miss M. McGarrity (now Mrs Fox), Mrs N. Conlan, Sister M. Bernadette, Sister M. Labourne (now Sr Bridie), Sister M. Teresita, Miss M. Teague (now Mrs Dolan), Miss A. Tomney (now Mrs McKenna), Miss M. McLaughlin, Miss I. Hagan (now Mrs McKenna), Mrs P. Foley, Miss N. McCaul (now Mrs McGarvey).

Six

The Railway

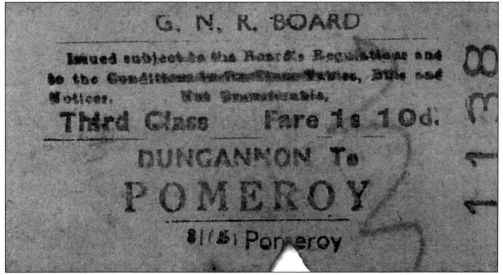

There was no talk of inflation when this rail ticket to Pomeroy was issued!

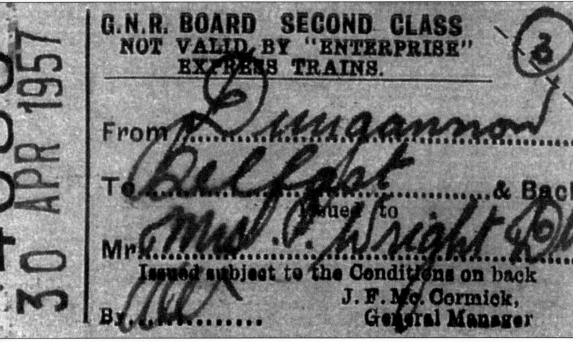

G.N.R. BOARD SECOND CLASS
NOT VALID BY "ENTERPRISE"
EXPRESS TRAINS.

From .... Dungannon ....

To .... Belfast .... & Back

Issued to

Mr .... Mrs .... Wright ....

Issued subject to the Conditions on back

J. F. Mc. Cormick,
General Manager

By ....

30 APR 1957

A ticket from the time when it was still possible to travel from Dungannon to Belfast by rail. The coming of the railway in the mid-nineteenth century, in the years immediately following the Great Famine, was a truly momentous event for the people of inland Irish counties like Tyrone. By 1858 the Great Northern Railway had extended the Derry line from Portadown to the outskirts of Dungannon. But the Earl of Ranfurly whose estate lay on the Portadown side of Dungannon refused to allow the railway to cross his land as he felt 'the belching monster' polluted the air, frightened cattle and horses and was a danger to man and beast. The matter was finally resolved, after much time and great expense, by digging a tunnel for one mile under the estate.

By 1860 the Derry line had extended beyond Dungannon to Donaghmore, Pomeroy, Carrickmore and the other stations *en route* to its destination. Since Pomeroy is the second highest village in Ireland, all the engineering expertise of the time must have been engaged on this part of the project. Between Pomeroy and Carrickmore the railway cut through high ranges of rocks, boulders and earth which had to be removed by manual labour and horse-drawn transport, not with the mechanization of today. What a mammoth task, and what a triumph its completion must have seemed to the people of the time for whom the 'iron horse' opened up a new world of travel. Little did those people think that in just over one hundred years that stretch of track would be lifted when the Portadown to Derry main line and all its branch lines were closed in 1965. The increase in road transport was given as the reason but politics as much as economics played a part in the decision.

The Great Northern Railway station in Dungannon.

Railway carriages parked outside Dungannon station in the early years of the twentieth century.

On 12 July 1900, Orangemen travelled by rail to celebrate in Carrickmore.

Donaghmore was the venue for the celebrations when these Orangemen arrived from Trew and Moy on a 'Special'.

Leaving Trew and Moy Station in July 1964.

Approaching Dungannon from the Portadown direction in 1964.

A goods train passes through Dungannon on its way from Portadown to Derry in 1964.

Looking towards Portadown from Dungannon station in August 1964.

The *Slieve Donard* leaving Dungannon for Belfast in August 1963.

The Derry to Belfast train enters Dungannon station for the last time in February 1965. No wonder a few sightseers turned out.

The Cookstown branch line outside Dungannon.

The platform at Dungannon for the Cookstown line.

Cookstown railway station as it once existed.

The Belfast to Derry train between Dungannon and Donaghmore in 1964.

The level crossing at Mullaghfurtherland, between Donaghmore and Pomeroy.

Steaming between Donaghmore and Pomeroy in June 1964.

A train enters Pomeroy station from Dungannon.

A view of Pomeroy station from the Dungannon side, as a Derry to Belfast train pulls in.

A Portadown to Derry goods train passes through Pomeroy in 1964.

Steaming through a valley between Pomeroy and Carrickmore towards the end of the rail era.